T0148295

PUTTING A STAKE IN THE GROUND

Strategies for Getting
Your First Marketing Journal Article
Published Successfully

Dr. Ken K. Wong

U21Global Graduate School | University of Toronto

iUniverse, Inc.
Bloomington

Putting a Stake in the Ground

Strategies for Getting
Your First Marketing Journal Article
Published Successfully

Copyright © 2011 by Ken K. Wong

iUniverse books may be ordered through booksellers or by contacting:
iUniverse
1663 Liberty Drive
Bloomington, IN 47403
www.iuniverse.com
1-800-Authors (1-800-288-4677)

ISBN: 978-1-4620-0021-0 (pbk)
ISBN: 978-1-4620-0020-3 (ebk)

Printed in the United States of America
iUniverse rev. date: 2/25/11

To my wife Winnie, and my family members
Hello Ma, Hello Dad, and Hello Chiu

Thank you for your love, understanding, patience, and confidence.

About the Author

Dr. Ken Kwong-Kay Wong

Dr. Ken K. Wong is a U21Global Marketing Professor and Subject Area Coordinator, training corporate executives and MBA students from over 70 countries. In 2008 and 2009, he received the Faculty Excellence Award, and was honoured in all three award categories, including: Outstanding Professor, Most Innovative Professor and Excellence in Online Education. Since 2003, Dr. Wong has been developing and lecturing marketing courses at the University of Toronto's School of Continuing Studies and also at various institutions of higher education in North America.

Dr. Wong's research interests include marketing for luxury brands, customer relationship management and online education. His articles have appeared in peer-reviewed international journals such as *Telecommunications Policy, Service Industries Journal*, and *Journal of Database Marketing and Customer Strategy Management*. Dr. Wong is also the author of the SCS lecture series in the areas of International Marketing, Advertising, PR & Publicity, E-Business, and Retail Merchandising. His latest work includes *Approved Marketing Plans, Avoiding Plagiarism, CRM in Action, More Bucks Annually,* and *Discovering Marketing in 38 Hours.*

Prior to entering the academic field, Dr. Wong was the Vice President of Marketing at TeraGo Networks (TSX: TGO) and had previously served as Director of eProduct Marketing at the e-commerce division of PSINet (NASDAQ: PSIX). He had also carried progressive product marketing roles at Sprint Canada and TELUS Mobility.

Certified by the American Marketing Association as a Professional Certified Marketer, Dr. Wong completed his Bachelor of Science degree at the University of Toronto and holds the International MBA degree from Nyenrode Business Universiteit in the Netherlands. He earned his Doctor of Business Administration degree from the University of Newcastle, Australia and has completed executive education programmes at both Kellogg and Queen's.

Table of Contents

Foreword

Ken Wong has provided an invaluable resource to all academics. While *Putting a Stake in the Ground* is particularly useful for doctoral students or junior faculty, it also serves as a reminder for senior faculty that the workings of a journal article are often a mystery for those first encountering it.

He has written an excellent guide for those young academics seeking to understand the process on their own as well as advisors who want to make sure they prepare their students for life as a scholar. He has filled a major gap, and done so with incredible coherence and clarity.

Professor Dipak C. Jain
Dean of INSEAD
Dean Emeritus of Kellogg School of Management

Preface

A common challenge faced by junior marketing faculty is to build a substantial track record of research within the first few years of appointment. This is often measured by the number of articles published in peer-reviewed academic journals. For tenure-track professors, the importance of publication cannot be ignored even if they have achieved a stellar teaching performance and fulfilled their daily administration duties. Recent research has confirmed that having good publication is a key criterion for faculty promotion. This is particularly true when a school or department is accredited by AACSB, AMBA or EFMD because these accreditation agencies usually require senior faculty members to engage in an active research program.

For some professors, getting a journal article published is a piece of cake because they have been doing that for years, and the principle "practice makes perfect" applies to writing papers. But what if your publication record is currently "zero" because you have just completed your PhD or DBA degree? Academic publishing can be mysterious because it is not being taught in most graduate programs. Furthermore, some supervisors do not spend sufficient time coaching their graduate students on the publishing process because the common perception is: "These smart kids will figure it out eventually!" If my guess is correct, many adjunct or assistant professors are struggling because they do not know where to start. As time goes by, the pressure to deliver publications increases, and this sets the writing bar even higher.

Since my core competency is in the marketing area, this book is written with junior marketing faculty members and doctoral students in mind. Although many of my students and colleagues have reviewed the materials presented in this book, I know it is not perfect; in fact, it is far from perfect. As a writer, I would like to receive your feedback on my work. Your suggestions greatly help shape the future edition of this book; so please do not hesitate to drop me an e-mail.

Dr. Ken K. Wong 黃廣基 博士

Ottawa, Ontario, Canada
Jan 31, 2011

e-mail: ken.wong@utoronto.ca
e-mail: kwong@u21global.edu.sg
Twitter: http://twitter.com/drkenkwong
Web: http://www.introductiontomarketing.ca/

Acknowledgement

In completing my book, I have drawn support from many people and thus feel a huge debt of gratitude. I would like to thank the International Editorial Board for providing me with valuable input and constructive criticism to my work.

International Editorial Board:

Abdalla Gholoum
Annie Nyet Ngo Chan
Basil Pathrose
Chee Wai Hoo
Dutta Bholanath
Ekaterina Leonova
Engelbert Atangana
LH Kho
Khurshid Jussawalla
Kishore Pai
Lothar R. Pehl
Narendra Nesarikar
Rajen Kumar Shah
Richard Anthony
Shama Dewji
Tasneem Tailor
Vicky Yan Xu
Vien Cortes
Zulfikar Jiffry

PART 1   Journal: An Introduction

Chapter 1 – Why Journal Articles?

Journals vs Magazines

Have you ever wondered how marketing professors keep up with their knowledge years after graduating from the university? In addition to reading newspapers or watching TVs, marketing professors who are on tenure-track, in general, spend a lot of time conducting research and reading peer-reviewed (refereed) marketing journals.

If my guess is correct, 99% of the general public would not spend time to read journals on a regular basis. This is because journals such as *Journal of Marketing* are often printed in black and write, have no photos, and the text is full of scientific calculations and formula that most people would have difficulty to comprehend. Do not confuse them with those colorful magazines that you can easily buy from your bookstores because they are not the same. In the past, people had to visit a university library to locate these journals. However, most of these journals are now accessible electronically over the Internet, or via your university's e-library. Although there is still a significant amount of journals that maintain both printed and electronic editions, more and more of them are now accessible via online subscription only.

Disseminating Knowledge with Journal Articles

Although these journals may seem to be boring to read, they actual play an important role in the academic community: They serve as a credible platform for knowledge dissemination. I know some of you will immediately argue that newer tools such as blogs, discussion forums, and web sites like Wikipedia can serve the same function to exchange information, however, the online content may not be trustworthy as anybody can post their thoughts virtually in a matter of seconds. On the other hand, articles in an academic journal usually undergo several rounds of reviews prior to publication. The journal editor acts as the gatekeeper to do the preliminary screening. Then, the paper is evaluated by 2 or 3 anonymous reviewers who are professors sitting in the editorial board of the journal. In most cases, a submitted article goes through several rounds of editing and the whole process may take several months to a year. Most of these journal articles cover original research conducted by the author(s). By sharing research results through these academic journals, advanced marketing knowledge is able to spread within the academic community around the world.

Professors are willing to spend years to conduct research and write papers because these research activities are part of their performance review. Like it or not, universities around the world are being ranked by the number of research output as appeared in top academic journals. The higher the ranking, the more funding a university can seek from the government. If it is a private university, a higher ranking usually means higher revenue because the university is able to attract top students who are willing to pay a premium in tuition fee in exchange for a prestigious degree.

If you are planning to be a marketing professor in the future, or a junior faculty member who is thinking of a tenure-track academic career, you need to know that getting your research findings published is important. Being a professor is not just about teaching. The other 2 areas of key duties include research and administration. Publish or perish, I can't stress how true this is!

How This Book is Organized

To set the stage for discussion, part 1 introduces you to the world of journal publishing. I will first compare the journal with other types of publications and then describe how it is ranked in the academic circle. Some potential publication outlets are shown for your consideration. I will also outline the criteria for journal selection that you should be aware of. Part 2 is all about the manuscript preparation. I will discuss the kinds of papers that you can write and give you some tips and tricks for your manuscript preparation. Since many authors are faced with the issue of having low-resolution graphics, I have dedicated a chapter to addressing this issue. Part 3 focuses on the process of journal submission. I will go through the submission steps in great detail and show you the remedies in the unfortunate event that your manuscript is rejected. The production process is presented in a step-by-step manner, and I will also share with you my insights on dealing with journal graphics designers and production coordinators. In the final part of this book, I will present to you some alternative publishing avenues in case you feel that journal publishing is not your cup of tea.

Getting your first marketing journal article published does not need to be stressful or painful. Let us put a stake in the ground to begin the writing journey and achieve your goals!

Chapter 2 – Ranking of Marketing Journals

The Ranking Game

There are hundreds of marketing journals out there in the market so how can you tell which one is the best? Whenever my colleagues or students ask me if I have heard about so and so journal, I often look them up using the guidelines as provided by these organizations. Each of the following rankings has its own methodology so you are highly suggested to consult a few of them in order to get an idea. In general, I don't see much discrepancy among these lists. If the journal that you are considering is a new one that only started publication in the last few years, it may not be included in the rankings.

When you go through these different journal rankings, you have to check the meaning of the number or alphabet presented. In some rankings, a "3" may suggest a third-class journal, while in others, it may mean the best, so you have to check out the ranking explanation carefully.

- **ABDC Journal List, published by Australian Business Deans Council, 2008**
  http://www.abdc.edu.au/3.43.0.0.1.0.htm

- **ABS Academic Journal Quality Guide, published by the Association of Business Schools (ABS), UK., 2009**
  http://www.the-abs.org.uk/?id=257

- **ERA Ranked Outlet, published by Australian Research Council (ARC), 2010**
  http://www.arc.gov.au/era/era_journal_list.htm

- **Journal Quality List, compiled by Professor Anne-Wil Harzing**
  http://www.harzing.com/jql.htm

- **Journal Recommendations for Academic Publication 2010, published by Cranfield University School of Management**
  http://www.som.cranfield.ac.uk/som/p10597/Research/Journal-Rankings

- **SCImago Journal & Country Rank**
  http://www.scimagojr.com

Ken's Journal List

If you do not have time to go through the above web sites, you can use the following list as a starting point. Frankly speaking, there is nothing wrong with the recognized or unranked journals that I have listed at the bottom of my list because they also have good quality articles. Many of them are just newer journals (i.e., with less than 10 years of history) that have not yet gained the global recognition they deserved, or have smaller distribution which negatively affected their market perception.

Tier-1 journals:

Journal of Marketing
Journal of Marketing Research
Journal of Consumer Research
Marketing Science

Well-respected, top journals:

Journal of Medical Marketing
International Journal of Research in Marketing
Journal of the Academy of Marketing Science
Journal of Interactive Marketing
Journal of Public Policy and Marketing

Journal of Retailing
Marketing Letters
Journal of Advertising
Quantitative Marketing and Economics
Industrial Marketing Management
Journal of Product Innovation Management

Respected journals:

Journal of Advertising Research
Journal of Personal Selling & Sales Management
Journal of Business Research
Journal of Macromarketing
Psychology and Marketing
Journal of International Marketing
International Journal of Electronic Marketing and Retailing
International Marketing Review
Journal of Services Marketing
European Journal of Marketing
Journal of Consumer Marketing
Healthy Marketing Quarterly
International Journal of Market Research
Journal of International Food and Agribusiness Marketing
Journal of Retailing and Consumer Services
International Journal of Internet Marketing and Advertising
Journal of Marketing Theory and Practice
Qualitative Market Research
Marketing Intelligence and Planning

Recognized journals:

International Journal of Bank Marketing
Journal of Marketing Education
The Service Industries Journal
Journal of Empirical Generalisations in Marketing Science
Journal of Business and Industrial Marketing

Journal of Marketing in Higher Education
Journal of Hospital Marketing & Public Relations
Journal of Marketing Communications
Journal of Business-to-Business Marketing
International Journal of Advertising
Journal of Food Products Marketing
Services Marketing Quarterly
Journal of Political Marketing
Journal of Global Marketing
Journal of Travel and Tourism Marketing
Advances in International Marketing
Journal of Pharmaceutical Marketing and Management
Marketing Management

Journals that are new, unranked, or have limited circulation:

Journal of Hospitality and Leisure Marketing
Journal of Marketing Channels
Advances in Consumer Research
Journal of Relationship Marketing
Journal of Promotion Management
Journal of Nonprofit and Public Sector Marketing
Journal of Euromarketing
Review of Marketing Science
Journal of Brand Management
Journal of Product & Brand Management (featuring Pricing Strategy & Practice)
Journal of Database Marketing and Customer Strategy Management
Journal of Strategic Marketing
International Journal of Sport Management and Marketing
Sales and Marketing Management
Marketing Research
ABA Bank Marketing
Australasian Marketing Journal
International Journal of Electronic Customer Relationship Marketing
International Review on Public and Nonprofit Marketing

Journal of Direct, Data and Digital Marketing Practice
Marketing Theory
Total Quality Management & Business Excellence
Marketing Bulletin
Journal of Targeting, Measurement, and Analysis for Marketing
International Journal of Business Science & Applied Management
International Journal of Technology Marketing
Journal of Retail Marketing Management

Chapter 3 – Which Journal to Choose?

Don't Crash Your Porsche!

In the last chapter, I have given you a pretty comprehensive list to begin your journal search. Should you target a top-tier journal for your first article submission? Well, unless you are 100% confident about your research and writing capability, aiming too high can be devastating. Some top journals are too popular that they receive hundreds of manuscript submissions a day. Your manuscript may either get rejected soon after your submission or get buried in the pile, meaning it can take up to a year or two before you hear anything from the journal editor. In some extreme cases, sending in a poorly written journal article may damage your reputation. You do not want the editors to chat among themselves and say something like, "Have you seen this crap from Dr. X?"

To give you an analogy, if you just got your driver's license recently, it may not be a good idea to choose a Porsche or a Ferrari as your first car because you are an inexperienced driver. Do you still remember how you got minor scratches on your first car while practising your driving and parking skills? The same can be said for journal writing and submission: most people make mistakes in their academic writing journey, so do not use your dream journal for practice.

The question about which journal to choose for your first manuscript submission is not that difficult to answer if you are willing to do a bit of homework. I can think of seven aspects that may influence your journal selection decision. They are:

1. School's Suggested List for Publication
2. Publication Frequency
3. Editor's Background
4. Author's Background

5. Article Type
6. Impact Factor
7. Readership Profile

I will discuss each of these criteria further in the next few pages.

School's Suggested List for Publication

The first step is to check with your dean or department head if the school has any list of suggested journal publications. This is because some schools can receive additional government funding and/or better national ranking if their faculty members have publications in certain journals. Hence, having an article published in one of the suggested journals may earn you merit points for promotion consideration. As such, it is vital for you to discuss your publishing plan with your supervisor and explore if such suggested publication list exists in your university.

Publication Frequency

Not all marketing journals are published on a monthly basis. Take a look at the following examples to see the variation in publication frequency.

- Journal of Retail Marketing Management: 2 issues per year
- Journal of Interactive Marketing: 4 issues per year
- Journal of Marketing: 6 issues per year
- Journal of Brand Management: 9 issues per year
- Service Industries Journal: 14 issues per year

In general, each issue will publish 4 to 10 original research articles. With this understanding, you can roughly calculate the number of articles that will be published. Assuming you have identified 5 or 6 journals that you want to target and all of those in your list have similar impact factor (academic importance), then selecting one that publishes more frequently may increase your chances of getting published.

Editor's Background

The editor-in-chief plays a key role in the journal's success. He or she is the gatekeeper and probably does all of the preliminary screening for all incoming manuscripts. Without the editor's blessing, your manuscript will not get moved up to the next evaluation stage by the reviewers. Therefore, it is important for you to find out who this editor is and figure out his or her evaluation criteria. For example, some editors only choose to publish papers that make use of traditional research methods that are sound and proven. Hence, if your paper uses some of the emerging statistical techniques, such as Partial Least Squares path modeling, it may get rejected easily because it does not use the traditional AMOS or LISREL method that the editor is familiar with.

If the same person has been serving as editor-in-chief for years, there is a high probability that this person is the founder of the journal; hence, you will not see any major change in the journal style and evaluation process in the near future. On the other hand, there are also journals that select a new editor-in-chief from its editorial board every few years. Therefore, comments from your colleagues such as "Journal X does not like to publish descriptive papers." may not be applicable anymore because the journal is now in the hands of a new editor-in-chief.

Author's Background

In addition to finding out who the editor is, I would also suggest that you observe the kinds of authors who have had their papers successfully published in the journal as this may give you some hints into the manuscript selection process. By definition, the peer-reviewing process should be anonymous because your manuscript should not include your name and affiliation. However, any experienced reviewer can honestly tell you that it usually takes only a minute or two to figure out who the author is from a basic Google search. The unfortunate reality is that the academic community is not fully immune to problems such as bias and discrimination. If there were only 1 available slot left for publication in the next issue of the journal, and the following 2 equally well-written articles were being evaluated, which one would you choose if you were the editor-in-chief?

Paper (A) –   written by a famous Kellogg marketing professor
Paper (B) –   written by an unknown professor who works in a
                university in a developing country

Despite the fact that virtually all academic journals state that they welcome manuscript submissions from academics around the world, some of them simply have a regional focus or give preference to papers coming from faculty members who teach in the same country or region. As a result, you should check the past several issues of your target journal to see if it really fits with your background.

Article Type

Some journals mainly publish original research articles, while others also publish book reviews and technical notes. You need to do your homework to understand the kinds of papers your target journal is looking for. The length of your article also matters. For example, *Marketing Letters* only publishes short papers that are under 20 pages, double-spaced. Hence, your masterpiece will be rejected if it is too long. In another example, the papers in the *Journal of Marketing Research* are highly technical, and most include advanced mathematical formulas. If yours is a descriptive one that does not include any formulas, I guess the probability of getting your paper published in the JMR would be low. Remember, each journal has its own manuscript requirements and restrictions; you must spend time checking them out on the publishers' web sites prior to submission.

Impact Factor

Once a research paper is published, how can one tell if it is more valuable than another article from the academic perspective? It is all about citation and referencing. The more an article is cited by others, the more valuable it becomes. The research firm Thomson Reuters scans through published papers electronically and publishes Journal Citation Reports to show the impact factor of each journal that it monitors. Basically, the more articles in a journal that are being cited by others, the higher the impact factor the journal can earn. Similar to the suggested publication list that I have mentioned earlier in this chapter, the impact factor can be used as a guide in choosing a journal for publication. Some schools simply set the impact factor threshold and say "You must publish in a journal that has an impact factor of X or above!"

The good thing about the impact factor is that it helps you compare the relative academic status of different journals easily. However, the impact factor (e.g., 0.283) can be meaningless if you consider it alone. Furthermore, this rating scheme only monitors a limited number of marketing journals. You can learn more about the Journal Citation Reports at:

http://thomsonreuters.com/products_services/science/science_products/a-z/journal_citation_reports

Readership Profile

Who is the target audience of your journal? Is it industry practitioners, government officials, professors, graduate students, or a combination of these? If your paper targets a journal that focuses on disseminating knowledge to people who work in the business sectors, your technical paper may not be suitable for publication unless you tune it down to simple English. Similarly, if the journal you want to have your paper published in is an advanced one, your paper may not be technical enough to be considered for publication. All of these mean that you need to have a clear understanding of the journal readership profile and then choose a suitable one for publication.

PART 2   Manuscript Preparation

Chapter 4 – What to Write?

The 8 Types of Journal Articles

The most common type of article that can be found in an academic journal is the original research article, in which researchers proudly present their research findings. However, many junior faculty members are not aware that journals also publish other kinds of articles in each issue. Technically speaking, a journal article can be categorized into one of the following 7 major types. Unless an exception is specified by the journal, all of these should be peer-reviewed by the reviewers anonymously.

1. Original Research Article
2. Case Study
3. Research Notes (Opinion Pieces)
4. Technical Notes
5. Book Review
6. Legal Update
7. Editorial
8. Rejoinder

   In the following pages, I will show you how these articles differ using examples.

Original Research Article

You have already conducted a research project during your PhD/DBA dissertation phase, so why not turn your hard work into an original research article that the world can view? It would be a waste to hide your excellent research work in the dissertation archive of your university library. Remember, like perishable food, your research data have a shelf life so you should not wait too long to revisit your 50,000-word dissertation. As long as your research topic is interesting and uses a robust research methodology, I think the global research community would like to hear from you.

If you have invented something totally new or made a breakthrough, that would be great. If you have found a way to improve an existing way of doing things, that would be fantastic as well. Although your research findings may not directly lead to the development of a commercial product or get you the Nobel Prize, your paper may inspire other researchers to conduct additional research and improve the world's knowledge of a particular topic. No matter how insignificant a research may seem to be, all original research articles have some value.

The best way to begin writing your research article is to first go through a few past issues of your target journal. Pay attention to the following aspects when you do your homework:

1. Citing and referencing styles: Is it APA, Harvard, Chicago, or a customized one?
2. Length of paper: focus on the actual word count of those published papers. Are they long, short, or a mixture of both?
3. Manuscript presentation: How do they show tables, graphics and formulas?
4. Are there any special requirements for the Abstract, Keywords, and Author Biography?

As a rough guideline, your research article should include the following elements:

- Abstract
- 5 to 8 Keywords
- Introduction
- Literature Review
- Research Methodology
- Data Analysis
- Conclusion (including managerial implications, limitations of the paper, and future research direction)
- Author's Biography and Contact Information

Here is an example of an original research paper:

Baxter, S. (2009). Learning Through Experience: The Impact of Direct Experience on Children's Brand Awareness. *Marketing Bulletin*, 20(2). Accessed on Nov 17, 2010. URL: http://marketing-bulletin.massey.ac.nz/V20/MB_V20_A2_Baxter.pdf

Case Study

Industry practitioners and academics can learn a lot by examining others' stories of failure or success. A case study is an article in which the researcher discusses a real-world case that relates to a particular topic, company, and/or event. Usually, a case study includes the following elements:

- Abstract
- 5 to 8 Keywords
- Introduction
- Background and Context (History and Latest Development)
- Problems/Challenges
- Handling of the Situation
- Impact Assessment (Financial and Strategic)
- Conclusion
- Author's Biography and Contact Information

Dr. Ken Kwong-Kay Wong

Here is an example of a case study:

Angelmar, R. (2007). The rise and fall of Baycol/Lipobay. *Journal of Medical Marketing*, 7, 77–88. doi:10.1057/palgrave.jmm.5050068. Accessed on Nov 17, 2010. URL: http://www.palgrave-journals.com/jmm/journal/v7/n1/full/5050068a.html

Research Notes (Opinion Pieces)

Some articles involve the proposal of new processes, new thinking, or new ways to get things done in the industry. Unlike a theory paper, which goes into a detailed technical discussion, a research note or opinion piece mainly contains the author's own view and justification. This kind of paper usually includes a detailed critique of the current methodology or situation. While the format of research notes varies a lot based on the topic being discussed, most include the following basic elements:

- Abstract
- 5 to 8 Keywords
- Introduction
- Proposal
- Justification for Change
- Applicability of New Process/Thinking/Framework
- Conclusion
- Author's Biography and Contact Information

Here is an example:

Illert, G. and Emmerich, R. (2008) Marketing Strategy: The need for new promotional models. *Journal of Medical Marketing*. 8, 23–30. doi:10.1057/palgrave.jmm.5050124 Accessed on Nov 17, 2010. URL: http://www.palgrave journals.com/jmm/journal/v8/n1/full/5050124a.html

Technical Notes

Through technical notes, researchers can help fellow researchers with the technical side of their work, such as by sharing tips and tricks in the use of a particular software. For example, Yam (2004) wrote an excellent article back in 2004 to show the research community how to make good use of MS PowerPoint to create high-resolution images. His article, below, can be accessed online:

Yam, C-S. (2004). Using PowerPoint to Create High-Resolution Images for Journal Publications. *American Journal of Roentgenology.* 185(1), p273. Accessed Nov 17, 2010. URL: http://www.ajronline. org/cgi/reprint/185/1/273.pdf

Another example of a technical note is:

Bound, J. (2009). User's Guide to DIRICHLET. *Marketing Bulletin.* Technical Notes 1. Accessed Nov 17, 2010. URL: http://marketing bulletin.massey.ac.nz/V20/MB_V20_T2_Bound.pdf

Book Review

With so many new books appearing in the market everyday, it can be challenging to keep up with the latest developments. A book review serves to introduce these great publications to the research community; the critique helps professors and researchers avoid picking up the wrong books. You do not have to be politically correct when writing a book review. If the book you are reviewing is a lemon, just say so. A typical book review covers the following items:

- Book Information (Book Title, Author, Editor, Publisher, Edition, Year, Pages, ISBN #, Price)
- 5 to 8 Keywords
- Introduction
- Target Audience

- Author's Background (Is he/she qualified to write the book?)
- Overview of the Chapters (Is any chapter is a must-read?)
- Conclusion (Is this a good book all in all? Is it too expensive? Too wordy? Boring?)
- Author's Biography and Contact Information

The following is an example of a book review:

Hay-Gibson, N. (2010). Book Review: Information Systems Management In Practice. *International Journal of Business Science and Applied Management*, 5(3). Accessed Nov 17, 2010. URL: http://www. business-and-management.org/download.php?file=2010/5_3--43-44-Hay-Gibson.pdf

Legal Update

As a marketer or a professor teaching a marketing subject, you need to be aware of the constantly changing macro environment, including changes in local laws and regulations. While newspapers may touch upon these changes from time to time, the depth of analysis in newspaper articles may not be sufficient from an academic point of view, plus the tone can be politically biased depending on who the publisher is. As such, some journals have dedicated a "Legal Update" section to provide a platform for researchers and professors to discuss legal changes and their implications to industry practices. A typical legal update covers the following items:

- Introduction
- Background and Context (History and Latest Development)
- Description of the Legal Changes
- Public Reaction
- Change Assessment
- Conclusion
- Author's Biography and Contact Information

The following article is an example of a legal update:

Nettleton, E. and Willison, C. (2010). Data protection: More powers for the information commissioner. *Journal of Database Marketing & Customer Strategy Management,* 17(2), pp 132-137. doi:10.1057/ dbm.2010.5 Accessed Nov 17, 2010. URL: http://www.palgrave-journals.com/dbm/journal/v17/n2/full/ dbm20105a.html

Editorial

In general, you will not have the opportunity to write an editorial piece for a journal unless you are one of the editors. However, when there is an urgent issue in the industry that needs to be addressed or a controversial debate that needs to be put to bed, editors may invite subject matter experts to write a joint editorial. A recent example of which can be found in the *MIS Quarterly,* in which the editor invited Professor Chin to comment on the general misuse of the PLS methodology among academics. This article can be found at:

Marcoulides, G.A., Chin, W.W., and Saunders, C. (2009). A Critical Look at Partial Least Squares Modeling. *MIS Quarterly.* 33(1), pp. 171-175. Accessed Nov 15, 2010. URL: http://www.misq.org/archivist/ vol/no33/issue1/ForewordPLS.pdf

Rejoinder

Perhaps the most interesting article to read is the rejoinder. The term refers to a piece written in response to a previously published article. An old saying goes: "If you like the article, cite it in your own work. Otherwise, write a rejoinder for rebuttal!"

Rejoinders are keys to the development of our knowledge. If you ever come across a rejoinder to your published article, you should actually be happy and not take it personally. This is because it may serve to point out a serious flaw in your research that you were otherwise unaware of. I have studied many rejoinders, and their outcomes are usually good – the release of an improved software, the correction of an embarrassing data analysis error, and/or a better understanding of the conditions in which a newly proposed methodology should be applied. While there is no common format for a rejoinder, it should at least cover the following aspects:

- Abstract
- 5 to 8 Keywords
- Introduction
- Overview of the Published Article
- Critique of the Published Article (Methodology and/or Data Analysis)
- Conclusion
- Author's Biography and Contact Information

Below is an example of a rejoinder:

Henseler, J. (2010). A Comparative Study on Parameter Recovery of Three Approaches to Structural Equation Modeling: A Rejoinder. *Social Science Research Network*. Accessed Nov 15, 2010. URL: http://ssrn.com/abstract=1585305

Chapter 5 – Quality Control

You spent months conducting your research and then weeks writing your masterpiece, so why are you rushing to submit the paper to a journal without doing any proper quality control? Yes, it may cost you time and money but a well-polished paper has a much higher chance of getting accepted by a journal than does a poorly written one. If you are serious about journal publishing, you simply cannot afford to ignore this important step prior to article submission.

Fixing Your English

I know it may sound insulting to some people, but the reality is that academically speaking, most of us write poorly. Yes, you may be a professional blog writer or a regular columnist in a school magazine or newspaper, but writing a journal article is different. It is like learning a foreign language. If you do not use the right terminology in your paper or do not follow specific journal writing rules, your paper will not be good enough for publication in a reputable academic journal. This issue is particularly true for junior faculty members whose mother tongue is not English.

The first step in cleaning up your grammatical errors is to do a spell check in your word processor. Then, see if your targeted journal has special instructions regarding the use of 3-em dashes, the Oxford comma, and straight quotes in the manuscript. Follow these instructions if given.

After that, ask a colleague at school to read your manuscript. If your colleagues are busy, consider hiring a local editor to proofread your work. A word of caution: Many people claim to know English language editing and offer such service at a cheap price, so choose a proofreader who is a native English speaker. If the editor of your target journal is based in the UK, find somebody who is good at writing British

English. Remember that there are still some noticeable differences among Canadian English, American English, British English, and the English commonly used in Asian countries.

What if you cannot find somebody locally who can be trusted to do the editing and proofreading of your manuscript? Well, the good news is that there are professional English editing service providers that target the academic journal publishing industry. One of the prominent service providers in this field is SPi. You can learn more about their service at http://www.prof-editing.com. In terms of turnaround, editing a 5000-word journal article takes about 2 weeks. The rate in the industry is about USD$0.032 per word.

Preparing Your Tables

In a manuscript, you often need to present data in table format. Before getting too excited, try to review several past articles from your target journal to understand how tables are usually presented. This will give you an idea of how tables should be designed and also saves you the trouble of having to reformat them later.

From my experience in dealing with journal publishers, I know that they often require that tables be saved separately from the manuscript, in either GIF or Microsoft Excel format. In other words, you should never include (embed) the tables within the manuscript itself. Even if you plan to upload the GIF files to the publisher's manuscript submission system, you should still keep your tables in a separate set of Excel files because this will definitely save you time down the road in case you need to regenerate the tables. I have encountered several incidents in which the journal's graphics designer needed my Excel files to generate the tables properly. You do not want to take the risk of having an outsourced typesetting provider retype all your important data during the desktop publishing process.

If you prefer to send your tables in graphics format, you can still do so. Once your tables are generated in MS Excel, use the "Save As..." function to save your current worksheet as a PDF file. If you are using a Mac, you can print the worksheet as a PDF file directly by clicking the PDF option in the "Print" menu. For Windows users, if the PDF function is not available in Excel for whatever reason, you can still convert your tables to PDF format indirectly by making use of the free "PrimoPDF" plug-in. If you need to enlarge the size of your table, you can change the fonts directly in Excel. A faster way is to open your PDF file, zoom in to make the table look bigger on-screen, and then do a screen capture.

Before you submit your manuscript, make sure that you have named the table files properly. Avoid spaces or special characters in the file names. Finally, review your manuscript one last time to ensure that tables are not embedded in the file itself and that you have indicated the approximate locations for the table insertions.

Preparing Your Figures

When I say figures, I am referring to drawings, charts and photos. The most common feedback that you will receive from a journal publisher is that your graphics files do not have the required minimum resolution for print publishing. In other words, your figures are not sharp enough. Your first reaction may be: "Are you kidding?" After all, you may be wondering why that is the case since you can view these figures clearly on your computer screen. Well, here is why: the computer screen can only show a maximum of 72dpi (dot per inch), so your figure looks amazingly clear on-screen. For traditional print publishing, you need at least 150dpi to pass the acceptable mark, and most publishers prefer that figures have at least 300dpi.

The multi-million question is, "How do I convert my 72dpi screen shot into a 300dpi file?" If I knew an easy way to do it, I would become a millionaire. While it is technically possible to do (I will show you how later), the process is not that straightforward and can be time-consuming. Plus, you will need to have pretty good Photoshop skills. Hence, you should remember the following rules when generating figures during your research:

1. Screen capture is BAD, as it only produces 72dpi images at best. Do not use screen capture unless you have no other way to save the figure.

2. In SPSS or other statistical software, once the figure is generated, try to save it as a PNG or TIFF file instead of doing a screen capture. Right-click your mouse over the figure to see the available saving options.

3. Make good use of the "Export Image", "Save As...", and "Advanced" functions, which may provide options to save your graphics file in a better and clearer format.

4. Avoid saving your figure in JPEG and GIF file format.

5. Save your figure at the highest graphics quality. For example, you may be able to choose your preferred graphics quality, such as "Poor, Average, Best, or Uncompressed", before saving a file. Choose "Best" or "Uncompressed" whenever possible.

   Furthermore, try to create your figures in gray scale instead of using fancy colors. This is because your figures may eventually appear in a journal that only prints in black and white.

Paper Title

Do you have a long title or a short one for your paper? Some journals have a word-count restriction for the title. Thus, it is highly suggested that you check the "Instructions for Authors" section in the journal web site. For example, in the following journal the word-count limitation for the paper title is 15 words:

http://www.tandf.co.uk/journals/journal.asp?issn=0264-2069&linktype=44

This word-count limitation applies to the full paper title (main + secondary), so the following paper has a total of 14 words in its title:

> Reacting to the demands of service work: emotional resistance in the Coaching Inn Company

Another thing to pay attention to is the use of capitalization in the paper title. Most journals discourage the use of the title case for the article title. Thus, the following example may not be appropriate:

> Tariff Type Selection, Usage Intensity and Satisfaction of Wireless Internet Customers: An Empirical Study Among Early Adopters in Canada

It is highly suggested that you review several past issues of your target journal to see how the paper title is treated in general.

Running Head

Some junior faculty members have not heard about this term, and that is quite normal. Basically, the running head is a shorter version of your paper title. It is printed across the top of the journal pages and usually consists of less than 50 characters including spaces. Using the above-mentioned paper title as an example, the running head may simply be:

> Wireless tariff type selection in Canada

Abstract

In any original research article, the first section that you see is the Abstract, which provides a quick summary of the article. Similar to the executive summary in a marketing plan, it serves to catch the reader's attention. If the journal is a popular one that receives hundreds of article submissions a day, your abstract may be the only piece of information that the journal editor reads during the initial screening process. As a result, your abstract should be concise, to the point, and written without any citations, for example, (Smith, 2011). Most abstracts have a word-count limit of 250 words, but I have seen some journals with a more stringent restriction of 150 words or less.

Although you have to tell people what you have done in your research in the Abstract, there is no need to include all of your important findings there. Once again, the purpose of the Abstract is to catch the readers' attention so that they will continue to go through your whole manuscript.

Keywords

During the manuscript submission process, you must identify 4 to 6 keywords for your manuscript. These keywords tags are assigned to your article for database indexing to help researchers locate your article. Hence, your choice of keywords is important. Try to think about what you would type in Google Scholar or ProQuest when you want to look for a paper that has similar content to your manuscript.

Unless the keywords are names, you should type them in lowercase. If you are asked to include the keywords in the manuscript you are submitting, they should appear after the Abstract and before the beginning of your main article. Keywords should have the same font size and alignment as the Abstract.

Manuscript Word Count

Generally speaking, your paper should be between 4000 to 6000 words. However, some journals, such as the *Journal of Database Marketing & Customer Strategy Management,* accept shorter papers with at least 2000 words. *Marketing Letters* also accommodates shorter papers.

If your manuscript is over 10,000 words, perhaps you can break it down into two journal articles. Read past issues of your target journal to get an idea about the approximate length of published articles. It would be a pity if your masterpiece gets rejected simply because it is way too long or too short.

File Format

Most journals prefer file submissions in Microsoft Word or LaTeX (http://www.latex-project.org) format. If you are using MS Word, save your manuscript in the older Word 97-2004 ".doc" instead of the newer ".docx" format because some online submission systems have not yet been updated to accept the latter. Meanwhile, some emerging marketing journals do not accept the traditional LaTeX file format, so you have to make it a point to check first.

I know some of you are die-hard Apple iWorks, Corel WordPerfect, and OpenOffice users. While you can use these word processors in preparing your manuscript, please remember to save your article as a ".doc" file prior to uploading it to the manuscript submission system. You can change the file format by using the "Save As..." function in your word processor. Do not take the chance of uploading something that the system does not recognize; this is not the time to show off your loyalty to your favorite word processor.

Text Formatting

Times New Roman (on PC) and Cambria (on Mac) are your friends. When preparing your journal manuscript, there is no need to use any fancy fonts or styles to impress the editor. Try to avoid using any font color other than black, or any fancy styles such as boldface.

In terms of spacing, it is strongly recommended that you use double-spacing, although 1.5 line spacing will not get your manuscript rejected.

In-text Citations & Referencing

This is actually a tough one. Although most marketing journals use the common citation styles such as APA, Harvard, or Chicago, some have their own custom styles that they strictly enforce on authors. Thus, you must carefully check the requirements of your chosen journal and take the time to go through your paper line by line to make any changes necessary to meet these requirements. You will seem very unprofessional if you do not follow their citation and referencing style.

Using an incorrect citation and referencing style would not only upset your journal editor but also affect the probability of getting your paper accepted. Some editors may think that you are not serious about seeking publication, as you did not follow their "instructions for authors". In some extreme cases, the editor may think that you are just trying to recycle a paper rejected by another journal that has a different citation style. For a quick overview of key citation examples, you may refer to the following sites:

1. APA Styles: http://www.apastyle.org/learn/tutorials/basics-tutorial. aspx
2. Chicago Styles: http://www.chicagomanualofstyle.org/tools_ citationguide.html
3. Harvard Styles: http://www3.imperial.ac.uk/library/ subjectsandsupport/referencemanagement/harvard

For detailed examples, and to learn about online tools and software that you can use to put together these in-text citations and references, please refer to my other book, *Avoiding Plagiarism: Write Better Papers in APA, Chicago, and Harvard Citation Styles.*

A Blinded Manuscript

A blinded manuscript is a paper that does not identify who the author is. What you should know is that even if you do not print your name anywhere in the paper, the word processing software may still give hints as to the authorship of the article during the file-saving process.

If you are using MS Word on a Mac, go to the Word menu and choose "Preferences..." Select the security icon and click the box "Remove personal information from this file on save" under "Privacy options." If you are using MS Word on a PC, go to the "Tools" menu, select "Options," and click the "Security" tab. Then, select "Remove personal information from file properties on save" and click OK. Another way to go about this is to go to the file properties section in your word processor to change your name and organization information. Double-check your headers and footers as well to ensure your name does not appear in the document.

Author Biography & Contact information

Depending on the journal's requirement, you may be asked to include your biography in a separate file or to type it manually into the online submission system. Either way, the author biography is presented in paragraph form and usually consists of less than 80 words. Your biography should generally include the following information:

- Your job title
- Your teaching/subject areas
- Career highlights and/or teaching awards
- Areas of research interest
- Prior work experience (if applicable)
- Key publications

Again, it is best to take a look at some past issues of your target journal to get an idea of how the author biography should be written, as the styles can vary a lot. In addition to the author biography, you will also need to provide your contact information as part of the submission process. This often includes your organizational affiliation (i.e. your university and department), your school's mailing address, and your phone number, fax number and e-mail address.

Cover Letter

Paper submission is a formal process so you have to write a short 1-pager to introduce yourself to the editor, and discuss briefly why the journal should consider publishing your masterpiece. Save your cover letter in MS Word. You will need to upload it as a separate file, or to copy and paste it onto the online submission system later.

The 16-point Quality Assurance Checklist

By now, you should know the key areas to pay attention to prior to your journal article submission. Use the following QA checklist wisely to create a better paper, modify it according to your target journal's actual submission requirements:

1. Spell-check was done.
2. My manuscript was proof-read by an English editor or a colleague.
3. A separate set of tables is saved in MS Excel file format.
4. All figures are in high resolution (150dpi - OK; 300dpi - best) and can be clearly seen in gray scale (black/white) printing.
5. The paper title is less than 15 words.
6. The running head is less than 50 characters.
7. The Abstract is less than 250 words.
8. Four to 6 keywords have been created.
9. My manuscript is about 4000 to 6000 words.
10. My work is saved in .doc file format.
11. My paper has double-spacing.
12. My manuscript uses 12-point Times New Roman or Cambria font.

13. The correct citation and referencing styles are used.
14. All traces of my name and affiliation have been removed from the paper.
15. I have created a separate file for the author biography and contact information.
16. I have written a short cover letter to go with my submission.

.

Chapter 6 - Fixing Your Low Resolution Figure

What to do with my 72dpi screen shots?

There are 3 options for fixing low-resolution figures:

1. Go back to the original statistical/graphics software to re-create them. Do not laugh; this may actually be quicker than playing around with Photoshop.

2. Use the "Big Screen" screen-capture option.

3. Use Adobe Photoshop, an expensive photo editing software

The decision on which option to use depends on the number of figures you need to fix and your Photoshop skills. Think about it; if you only need to fix a few files and that you have your data set on hand, it might be easier to just recreate the graphics files using SPSS or Excel. If the original data set is not handy with you, then you can try the "Big Screen" screen-shot option that is described below.

The "Big Screen" Screen-capture Option

1. Use a large external monitor, unless you have a 17" laptop screen.

2. Double-click your graphics file. In theory, it will open in your system's default graphics preview or editing program.

3. Enlarge the window size of your figure to its maximum. Usually, you can do this by dragging the lower right-hand corner of your file

window further down to the lower right side of your screen. The figure will remain the same size but the white or gray background will become bigger.

4. Now, enlarge your figure. In some programs, you just need to click the "+" zooming icon or the "+ magnifying glass" icon on the tool bar. In other programs, you need to choose the "View --> Zoom In" function on the menu bar.

5. The enlarged figure now fills the big screen.

6. Do a screen capture of this super-large figure as usual. Choose "No compression" or "Best" quality if possible. Now your screen shot is done.

The file size of this newly created screen shot will be much larger than that of your original graphics file, but this is alright. You DO NOT need to do any resizing. The journal publisher's computer-based manuscript submission system will take care of making your huge file look good in the PDF proof that it will generate online. Also, resizing your large image is a piece of cake for a graphics designer, so there is no need to worry. The resulting figure that is fixed/resized by the publisher will have about 150dpi resolution. While it is still below 300dpi, it is at least better than your original 72dpi screen shot.

The "Photoshop" Option

If you already have the Photoshop photo-editing software installed on your computer, you can give the following method a try:

1. Launch your Photoshop program.

2. Create a high-resolution blank file. Go to "File" --> "New" and set the file resolution to 300. The width can be 5 inches, and the height 4 inches. Choose a white background, and just keep the file name

as "Untitled-1". When you are done, press the OK button.

3. While keeping this blank file open, go to the file menu to open your current low-resolution figure. Let us assume that your low-resolution file is titled "Figure5". Now, you should have 2 windows (or 2 tabs in 1 window) open on your screen.

4. Go to the "Figure5" window, and click on the Select icon in Photoshop to copy the whole figure. Then click the "Untitled-1" window and paste your figure there.

5. You may notice that your figure looks much smaller in the "Untitled-1" window. Do not worry. Just go to the lower left-hand corner to change the view percentage to 100%.

6. On the "Untitled-1" window, click on the Crop icon in Photoshop to crop out the extra white or gray background. Because your newly created file was originally made for 300dpi, Photoshop will increase the figure resolution during the copy-and-paste action.

7. At this point, your "Untitled-1" window should look similar to your old "Figure5" window. Save your "Untitled-1" file as "Figure5High" by going to "File" --> "Save As..." and choose "TIFF" as the file format. Now you have created a 300dpi figure from your original low-resolution file!

When I tried this method, my 37k sample file (in 72dpi) turned into a 1.1M file (in 300dpi). The Photoshop magic made it suitable for journal submission! Having said that, this process does not make your figure looks better. If your original 72dpi figure is burry, your newly created 300dpi figure will still look burry.

Part 3 Manuscript Submission

Chapter 7 – How to submit a research paper to a journal?

Submission Should Be Free

The submission process can be easy or difficult depending on your chosen journal. However, one thing for sure is that submission to internationally recognized journals is free of charge. Never pay any publisher to "evaluate" your paper submission or "complete" the document typesetting process because these should be free among reputable marketing journals. If you need extra help polishing your English or fixing your tables/figures, the publisher will usually refer you to third-party service providers because most publishers do not provide these chargeable services themselves. If you see a statement on a journal web site suggesting that you need to pay a certain fee to get your paper published, there is a high probability that the journal is a scam. Once your paper is accepted, you may decide to purchase some print copies of the journal from your publisher, but that is another story. In other words, having your manuscript submitted, evaluated, formatted, published online, and distributed to major databases should be totally free of any charge.

The Open Access Journals

The only exception to what I have just mentioned is the "author fee" (a.k.a. open access fee), which is commonly found in some open access (OA) journals such as Oxford Journals (http://www.oxfordjournals. org/oxfordopen). In recent years, some journal publishers have changed their business models to allow the public to freely download research papers from their web sites. For a list of these OA journals, visit the directory of open access journals (http://www.doaj.org).

Since these journal publishers do not accept advertisements, they have to turn to the authors for monetary assistance, which ranges from a few hundred dollars to three thousand dollars per article. You can find additional information on this matter at http://www.lib.berkeley. edu/scholarlycommunication/oa_fees.html.

As an author, you need to first ask yourself why you would want to publish your masterpiece in these open access journals, especially since you have to pay for your paper to be published and considering that these journals are usually not the top-ranked ones. My advice is that you consider OA journals only if you do not like the 80+ journals mentioned in Chapter 2. If I were you, I would use the money to source a good set of data for my next research paper instead of using it to pay to have my article published online.

The Half-baked Cake

One of my students asked, "Can I submit a half-completed paper to a journal?" No. You should only submit your paper when you believe that it is ready for publication. Any submissions with missing diagrams, tables, or text will automatically be rejected by the editor immediately in general. If you have an uncompleted, work-in-progress paper that you want to share with the academic community, you should do it via presentation in an academic conference, in the form of a "poster" or "short paper". Only send in your completed "competitive paper" for journal submission.

Am I authorized?

In the previous chapter, I have shown you the areas that you need to pay attention to when preparing your manuscript and associated files. Even when you have all of the files ready, you still need to ask yourself the following question prior to officially starting the submission process:

"Am I authorized to submit the article?"

This question seems weird considering you are the author of the manuscript. However, if your paper includes a figure, a table, or some data that have already been published elsewhere in the academic or commercial world, you must seek approval from the copyright holder of these contents prior to your journal submission. This is because you are now transferring the copyright of your whole article to your journal publisher. If your diagrams or tables have been previously published in conference proceedings that have subsequently been turned into a commercial book, you will need the approval of the original publisher to be able to use the same information.

Another situation in which you may not be authorized to submit the paper is when you are not the main (corresponding) author in a joint research. If your PhD supervisor is the main author, you must first get his/her approval, and it would be best to have it in writing. Otherwise, the main author may decide to submit the manuscript to another journal, or make adjustments to it at the last minute. As a result, it would best to let the main author handle the journal submission unless you are authorized to do so on his/her behalf.

Submit Your Manuscript via the Online Submission System

Sending your files to the journal can be easy or difficult. If your journal is using an online manuscript submission system, you will probably need 30 to 45 minutes to go through the paper submission process. First, you need to register on their site in order to open an author's account. Then, wait for the confirmation e-mail and click the activation link there. Once your account is set up, you can proceed to upload your files one-by-one. Some systems may allow you to select up to a maximum of 3 files per upload but it can still be a time-consuming process. You also need to arrange the file sequence and rename your files properly. The system will generate a PDF file for your review and sign off, once all of these files are uploaded properly into the system.

One of the common mistakes that authors make during submission is forgetting to approve the final computer-generated PDF. Often, you need to go back to the main menu of the submission system and view your pending activities. This is where you need to manually "approve" the PDF to complete the submission process. Once this is done, the online submission system sends you an e-mail to acknowledge your recent article submission. If you do not receive such e-mail within the day of submission, you probably missed some submission steps that require your attention.

Do not under estimate the amount of time you need to complete the submission process. You are bound to face technical issues during the process, so you not only need to set aside enough time but also be in good mood to do it. My advice is that you get yourself a cup of coffee or tea, find a comfortable chair, and turn off your annoying Skype/MSN connection before starting the journal submission process.

Submit Your Manuscript via E-mail

Some journals have a much easier submission process. All you need to do is to e-mail your files (cover letter, text, tables, and figures) to the editor and that's it! This is very common in journals that are fairly new, or those journals that are running by professors/departments that have little budget or IT resources. If your files are large, try to compress them into a single zipped file that is under 5MB. If your file is too large to send via e-mail, I would suggest you contact the editor for advice. He or she may send you a FTP link for direct file upload into their system, using an FTP client software such as WS_FTP (on a PC) or Fetch (on a Mac).

A good journal editor will typically send you an acknowledgement e-mail within several days of your submission. Since you are not using an online submission system, do not expect an immediate e-mail response from the editor. If you do not receive such acknowledgement e-mail within a week, send the editor a courteous e-mail to ask for confirmation. Remember, editors are often busy professors like you, so conduct yourself professionally, especially when your e-mail submission is made during the peak examination time. If you are sending out your manuscript during a public holiday (e.g., March break or Christmas), it is normal that the editor may not get back to you for another 2 or 3 weeks as he/she may be faced with a tsunami of e-mails after the holiday.

Submit Your Manuscript via Postal Mail

Yes, some journals still accept submissions via postal mail even though we entered the digital age more than two decades ago. Some older journals may also still allow you to save your work on a floppy disk, CD-ROM, or USB stick and mail it to the editor's office, which is usually his/her department in the university. Do not expect the editor to return these materials to you, so remember to save a copy for yourself! As you can imagine, it takes time to process these snail mails, so do not use this method unless all other submission methods have been exhausted. Contact the editor by phone to discuss your unique needs. Perhaps there are better ways to send in your work than through postal mail.

"Can I still send out manuscript that is handwritten?" That is probably not a good idea. Even if it were possible, the editor may charge you for the typing of your manuscript into MS Word. Plus, you do not want to take the risk of having embarrassing typo errors inadvertently included in your masterpiece.

The Waiting Game Begins

Once your manuscript and related files have been submitted to the journal, the waiting game begins. Unfortunately, the waiting time varies drastically among marketing journals. It depends on the editor, the volume of incoming manuscripts, and also the availability of peer reviewers. Remember, these editors and reviewers are professors or senior industry practitioners who only volunteer their time to work for the journal. They are not being paid to review your work. It may take a top-tier journal up to a year or even two to evaluate your work, so do not be alarmed if the waiting seems long. On the other hand, some newer journals may have aggressive timelines and thus have your manuscript evaluated within a few weeks. Hence, you need to make your choice wisely. Unlike a typical commercial service, there is no service level agreement (SLA) in journal publishing that you can hold the editors accountable for. In any case, if your paper is poorly written, the journal editor may get back to you within a few days of submission to give you the bad news that your paper has been rejected.

In my experience, it is reasonable to ask the editor for an update if you do not hear a decision on your paper 9 months after your submission. There is always the possibility that your paper has gotten lost in the pile and did not reach the intended reviewers. In some cases, the delay in the decision is caused by the different views of the reviewers. For example, if reviewer "A" believes that your paper is good and warrants publication, but reviewer "B" says your paper is worthless and has major methodology flaws. In such case, the editor may need to find a third reviewer to give your paper another look, or he/she may have to go through your manuscript in detail to make a final decision.

Chapter 8 – Feedback From the Editor

My Paper was Rejected

When the bad news arrived, relax and take a deep breath. First of all, you should understand that most journals have a rejection rate of 70% or more, so you are not alone. One of the reasons for rejection is that your research topic or theme does not "fit" with the objective of the journal. If the editor is nice, he or she will give you some suggestions on the possible publishing outlets that you can consider for future submission.

Another possible reason for rejection is that you have got some serious flaws in your research methodology. In this case, the editor will usually forward you a copy of the reviewers' report for your consideration. Other common reasons for rejection include:

- Data are too old (5+ years)
- Little academic contribution (everybody already knows about your findings)
- Poor English (the paper is unreadable)
- Plagiarism (Did you copy and paste a major chunk of text from elsewhere?)

Don't Burn the Bridge

Manuscript evaluation can be a highly subjective matter, so you should never get too frustrated with the editor and peer reviewers. Remember, the people who serve as peer reviewers are probably colleagues or friends of the editor, so bad-mouthing the reviewers in front of the journal editor will not do you any good. What you should do after receiving the rejection letter is to send a nicely worded response to the editor, thanking him or her for showing interest in your research topic and arranging a peer review of your paper. Unless you are certain that you will never meet these editors or peer reviewers in the future, do not let the professional relationship turn sour. In other words, do not burn the bridge. You may have lost this battle but not the war.

What to Do Next?

Getting a paper rejected is not the end of the world. What you should do is examine the reason of rejection and improve your manuscripts if required. Sometimes, there is nothing wrong with your paper; you have just chosen a top-tier journal that is out of your league, or you have selected a popular one that has to reject your paper due to limited publication space. Most journals publish 5 to 10 papers per issue so it is not uncommon for them to turn away some good ones when they are getting hundreds, if not thousands, of submissions from all over the world! There are many good journals out there so go through the list of journals that I have presented earlier, and choose another one to begin your submission process again!

My Paper Needs Revision

Most accepted articles went through one or more rounds of revision by the author. If the reviewers have questions about your paper, try to take time to address them properly one-by-one. Usually, getting questions from the reviewers is a good sign as it indicates that your paper is likely to be accepted. Think about it, if the paper is that bad, who is going to waste time to ask you questions for clarification; the editor would just send you a rejection letter right away!

Check with the editor regarding the revision timeline. In general, authors are given approximately two months to complete their revision. If you submitted your original article via an online submission system, the re-submission deadline for your revised paper is typically indicated online, so check carefully. If the deadline is too close, ask for an extension (e.g., a month or two) from the editor. This is a common request, so there is no need to feel shy about it. Of course, you have to justify your request for extension. Do you need extra time to revisit your original data set? Are you physically sick? Are you currently on vacation? Just be honest when dealing with the editor.

Dealing with the Graphics Designer

If you have been notified by the editor that your paper is accepted, congratulations! Does it mean that the mission is completed? Not yet! The fun actually starts, as you now need to deal with another group of people, namely, the graphics designer, the typesetters, the proofreader, and the production coordinator of the publisher.

Nowadays, most of these tasks are actually carried out by the publisher's team offshore in India or the Philippines because of their specialty in this area. If the publisher is a large one, you will be assigned a new username and password to access their publishing workflow system that is different from the manuscript submission system.

Once the design team completes the desktop publishing work of your article, you will be asked to download and proofread your article. This is the most time-consuming process because you now have to check your paper line-by-line, page-by-page to spot out any errors. Think about it, your research paper is being formatted into the appropriate journal format by the graphics design team who may have little knowledge about your research area. These designers do not hold PhD degrees in your field, so typesetting mistakes happen all the time. It is your responsibility to tell the designer what to do with your manuscript.

Areas for Checking

During the designing stage, you may be asked to review your manuscript several times. Please pay attention to the followings when checking your work:

1. Missing or incorrect caption/title of your figures. This is because

they are often manually re-typed by the graphics artist.

2. Incorrect spacing of text in your tables. Everything may look perfectly alright in your original Excel spreadsheet but don't forget that your table is now being reformatted into Adobe InDesign or other DTP program format. Can you see all of the text in the table? Are they in the right location? Has your "September 2010" suddenly turned into "Sep-10"? These are things that you should look out for.

3. Color of your graphs. If you are showing lines or bars in the chart, can you tell their differences? Is the color too light or dark? You may be able to get the graphics artist to adjust the "contrast" to make them look more attractive.

4. Typos. Your text from the manuscript is being "copied and pasted" or re-typed during the typesetting process. It is common to see typos in your proof. Pay special attention to the reference section.

5. Special characters and trademarked names. The typesetters may use some kind of spell check program on your manuscript and the computer program may accidentally change some of your special wordings. For example, "@Work" may become "At Work", "3G Wireless" may become "3 G Wireless", "LaTeX" may become "Latex" and "3,5$" may become "$3.50". Remember, this design team may not be located in your country so there's no common sense involved when applying changes to the manuscript.

6. Your text. Some publishers have in-house English editors and proofreaders in their graphics design department. Even without giving you prior notification or seeking your approval, they may have your manuscript "fixed" to make the sentences read better. Again, since the editor is not a subject matter expert in your area, there is a possibility that a key message, quote, or figure in your manuscript may be changed and its meaning altered.

7. Your biography and contact information. By the time your

manuscript reaches the graphics designer, it may be a year or two after your original submission date. Have you changed your university affiliation? Do you still use the same e-mail address and phone number? Update your biography accordingly if necessary.

The fact is that once you have approved the proof, the manuscript will be locked down in the system, meaning no more changes are allowed. Thus, take the time to double check your work before sending in your approval to the publisher.

Chapter 9 – Locating Your Published Article

Volume, Issue, and Page Assignment

What happens after the design work of your article is completed? Well, your article will join the queue for volume/issue assignment by the editor. Even though your article may have significant contribution to the academic and research community, the editor may decide to hold off its publication because the next issues are already full. This happens particularly when an upcoming journal issue is designated as a "Special Issue" dedicated to specific topics. It is highly possible for an article to appear in print edition of the journal 6 months or even longer after it has been accepted.

Articles in Press

Although your article may not immediately appear in the print copy, it is usually shown on the journal's web site, under the "Articles in Press" section, within a month after all the graphics design work have been completed. The publishing group Taylor & Francis calls this the "iFirst" system. A digital object identifier (DOI) is usually assigned to your article once it is published online. That means other people can immediately cite your article officially even if it is not yet shown in the print edition of the journal. For example, one of my papers that reached the "Articles in Press" stage can be cited as follows:

> Wong, K. K. (in-press). Fighting churn with rate plan right-sizing: A customer retention strategy for the wireless telecommunications industry. *The Service Industries Journal*, doi: 10.1080/02642060903295669.

When this paper finally received its volume, issue, and page assignment from the publisher, its citation became:

> Wong, K. K. (2010). Fighting churn with rate plan right-sizing: A customer retention strategy for the wireless telecommunications industry. *The Service Industries Journal*, 30(13), pp 2261-2271.

To locate any online journal article that has been given a DOI, go to http://dx.doi.org. Once you have entered the DOI information, wait for at least 10 seconds to give time for the system to resolve your enquiry.

Locating Your Article Online

There are two places in which your article will appear online:

1. The journal's web site
2. An online database

Having your article published on the journal's web site does not mean that other people can view your article in full. Very often, the journal will only show the title and abstract of your article. If people want to download your article or view it in full, they have to pay the publisher for it. In short, the publisher is selling your research article. Most journal publishers will send you an author's version of your article free of charge. While you may not be allowed to show the file in your department biography page, this free PDF of your article comes in handy when you want to share your success with your colleagues or dean.

The second place where your article can be found is in an online database such as ProQuest, EBSCOhost, InfoSci, Emerald Management First and ScienceDirect. The problem with this is that many journals enforce a 1- or 2-year embargo on their recent articles on these databases. While it is a good business strategy for making money (as others have to pay for recent articles at a premium, say USD$30 for each paper downloaded), this arrangement makes it virtually impossible for other researchers to access your manuscript, allowing them only a view of the abstract. As a result, you are likely to receive e-mails from other researchers asking if you are willing to send them a copy of your paper for their review, as they cannot find your manuscript in their online database subscriptions at school.

Locating a Physical Copy of Your Article

There are two ways to get hold of a print copy of your journal; you can either source one from the publisher or find a copy in your school library provided they have a subscription to your journal. Some publishers will send you a few copies of the journal upon your request. If you plan to buy physical copies of your article, try to do it as soon as your paper is accepted by the journal. This is because you will typically be offered an attractive author's price prior to the publication of the issue. Once the journal issue is printed, you have to pay the same published price to get your copies.

Finding a print copy of your article in the school library can be a challenging task. This is because more and more libraries are trying to save money by moving away from subscription to printed journals. However, it will not hurt to check with your librarian to see if the library can place a special order for you. This is typically possible if you are teaching a related course and intend to use the article as a case study. I cannot guarantee that this will work at your university, but there is no harm in asking.

PART 4 Beyond Journal Publication

Chapter 10 – Conference Proceedings

A Stepping Stone to Journal Publication

As I have pointed out earlier, it is important for professors to get some publication out during their academic career. However, it is very difficult to get into top journals and the evaluation process often takes months to years. So, is there an alternative way to get some peer-reviewed publications out earlier?

Yes, and they are called conference proceedings. In fact, many young researchers begin their publication journey by participating in academic conferences and have their "work-in-progress" papers published in the conference proceedings. Please note that some conferences do not publish proceedings so you have to choose the right one to participate carefully. Conference proceedings come in many formats, it may be a CD-ROM full of papers in PDF format, a special issue in a journal, or an edited book published by a commercial publisher.

Similar to journal papers, all conference papers are peer-reviewed as well. However, the evaluation turn around time is much faster; you will probably hear back from the conference chair within a month or two. Your paper may get accepted right the way, or need further editing as per the reviewer(s)' suggestion.

Getting a paper accepted at a conference can be a little bit easier and faster than getting it accepted in a reputable peer-reviewed journal. Because of this, some universities give relatively little credits to the conference proceedings as compared to journal articles for tenure decision. Is it better to have 1 article in a top-tier journal than having 10 conference proceedings? I do not know the answer to this, and you are highly encouraged to check with your dean or department chair. Having said that, not everyone can get published in a top-tier journal during the pre-tenure appointment period. In my opinion, having some publications is definitely better than having a "zero" publication record.

Different Kinds of Conference

There are many academic conferences in the market, and they are of different natures and reputations. Some conferences focus on a specialized field of marketing. For example, you may come across a conference that focuses specifically on Direct Marketing. Others serve a particular industry, such as education or medicine. On the other hand, there are conferences that welcome all kinds of marketing papers as long as these fit into one of the themes or tracks they have planned for the year.

Most conferences require the author to present his or her paper in person. This means you have to physically go to the conference venue to present your paper. Having said that, some conferences allow the author to "present in absentia" his or her accepted paper. While you may not enjoy experience of presenting in front of a group of professors and graduate students, such conference presentation is welcomed by those whose research and travel budgets have been drastically cut in recent years. Finally, do not forget that the virtual conference is no longer a myth. The university where I teach organizes a virtual business conference every year and accepts papers from researchers around the world. With this understanding, you have to choose carefully before sending in your paper for evaluation.

Type of Conference Papers

The types of conference papers that are accepted vary among different conferences. Typically, a conference papers falls into one of the following categories:

1. Full Research Papers

This research paper has single spacing and is about 8 to 10 pages long, including the appendix and references. It is not uncommon to see some professors present their competitive papers in a conference to get feedback from the academic community for the purpose of further fine-tuning their work.

2. Concise Papers

This paper is much shorter at approximately 4 to 6 pages, including the appendix and references.

3. Posters

With regard to poster presentations, you may be given some physical board spaces to post your key research findings. The content may be published in poster proceedings, although this is not common. No matter what kind of papers you are submitting, always check with the conference chair to learn about the type of publication that will be arranged for the accepted papers.

Tips on Submission

Similar to journal submission, most conference submissions require the author to set up an online account at the conference management system (e.g., EasyChair). Some registrations require the conference chair to manually approve your registration, so it may take a few days and some back-and-forth e-mails to complete the registration process.

It is well known among experienced conference participants that the paper submission deadline is often extended for a period ranging from 2 weeks to a month. While this practice is common, you are highly urged to submit your paper on time because the chair may decide not to grant an extension when there are sufficient good papers accepted.

Another point worth noting is that each conference usually has a specific theme or track for the year. Thus, if you can modify your paper accordingly to fit such theme or track, the probability of getting your paper accepted will increase. Although most conferences are run regularly, it is possible that the one you are considering may not get organized this year. Hence, you must not wait too long before submitting your paper because once you miss the deadline (and the subsequent extension), there is no guarantee that you can submit the same within the next 12 months.

One Paper, Two Submissions?

A common question from my student is: "Dr. Wong, if my paper has already been published in conference proceedings, can I still submit the same article to another conference or journal for publication?" Well, the answer is "No" because the conference proceedings is treated as publication that has its own copyright. Having said that, some journals allow you to submit a paper that has been totally re-written and expanded based on what you have presented in the conference. Check with the editor of your chosen journal early on to avoid disappointment because different journals have different policies on this matter. Also, you may need to seek written approval from the publisher of the conference proceedings especially if you intend to recycle some of the figures or tables in your subsequent journal submission.

Chapter 11 – Alternative Publishing Outlets

Professional Magazines

Unlike journal articles and conference proceedings, which are peer-reviewed, magazine articles are usually reviewed only by the editor. There are many marketing-related magazines on the market, the majority of which are published by marketing associations at the national level. For example, the American Marketing Association publishes *Marketing News* magazine on a monthly basis. In Canada, the Marketing Research and Intelligence Association publishes *Vue* magazine 11 times a year. These professional magazines usually have a theme for each month, and they typically post it in advance on their web sites. If you are not sure about whether your article is suitable for publication, always e-mail the magazine editor for clarification.

Since professional magazines are meant for business professionals and not just for academics, you cannot just submit your journal paper to a professional magazine for consideration. At the very least, you should pay attention to the following areas when preparing your manuscript:

1. Number of words: The paper should be 1000 words or less.

2. Conclusion: Instead of having it at the end of your article, present the conclusion at the beginning.

3. Citation style: None; that is, no in-text citation like (Smith, 2010) nor a long list of references at the end.

4. Footnotes and endnotes: These are not used in a magazine article.

5. Copyright: The magazine keeps the copyright, so you must not recycle any figures or tables that have been previously published in another magazine, journal, or conference proceedings.

6. Figures and Photos: Colorful ones are preferred.

Do not make the wrong assumption that a magazine article submission will easily get accepted. Unlike a journal, which focuses mainly on academic contribution, a magazine also considers whether your content can keep its readers interested and its advertisers satisfied. Hence, you have to think twice whether you really want to write an article for a professional magazine. Furthermore, magazine articles are not peer-reviewed so it may add little, if any, value to your publication portfolio.

Book Chapter in an Academic Volume

For some professors, the best way to "recycle" a rejected journal paper is to have it published as a chapter in an academic volume. This refers to books that are put together by academic book publishers such as Springer, IGI Global and Pearson Prentice Hall. From time to time, these publishers post a "Call for Chapters" proposal on their web sites along with the titles of the proposed volumes. What you need to do is to contact the specified volume editor and send in your manuscript for evaluation. Some of these academic volumes are peer-reviewed as well. Unlike a typical trade book, for which you can get 10% to 20% of the selling price as royalty, an academic volume does not pay any royalty to the authors; it only provides a small token, such as a $100 book certificate.

Trade Books

This is a tricky one. Technically speaking, anybody can publish anything on the Internet or make use of print-on-demand (POD) service providers to create a tangible book on any topics. Hence, a book publication is usually evaluated by the school using the following criteria:

1. Publisher: Is the book coming from a reputable publisher or a POD one?

2. Academic Contribution: Does the topic have any academic value? Can it be used as a textbook or supplementary study guide in any course?

3. Popularity: How many copies of the book have been sold or downloaded?

Having said that, writing a book is not as easy as one might imagine. In general, a decent book should have at least 10000 words, and it takes a lot of thinking, planning and writing to produce. If you plan to approach a traditional book publisher, expect to wait up to 2 or 3 years before seeing your book in print. This is mainly because book publishers typically already have a full production schedule for the year. Even if your book proposal gets accepted, it will still be queued up in the production pipeline, fighting for internal resources against other book projects. The rejection rate for a book proposal can be very high, especially if you are a new author in the industry.

Epilogue

Submitting an article to a journal for consideration can be an exciting yet challenging task. I still remember how I burned the midnight oil to meet submission deadlines and how much time I spent looking for the ideal publication outlet. My advice is that you consult with your colleagues and deans because they have firsthand experience on how to get a paper successfully published. As you have probably learned from your writing journey, there is always room for improvement in your paper. Hence, do not wait forever because your data set and analysis may be less relevant by the time you finish preparing your masterpiece. Put a stake in the ground to start your journal article writing and submission process.

Another point that I want to make is that having a paper rejected by a journal is a common thing. As I have discussed in this book, there are many possible reasons for such rejection, so you should simply consider the valuable feedback from the reviewers, revise your manuscript, and move on to find another publishing opportunity. Remember, the law of supply and demand also applies to the journal publishing industry.

I also want to stress the importance of having a good attitude and a lot of patience throughout your academic writing journey. There are no shortcuts in this endeavor. Never attempt plagiarism in your work, and always respect the publishing timelines that the journal editors and reviewers follow. As they say, "When in Rome, do as the Romans do!"

To those who are browsing this book right now at Chapters/Indigo, just pay for it and evaluate the book leisurely at home for 2 weeks. Do not stand in the aisle for the whole afternoon! Remember to keep your original receipt if you intend to get a full refund at the bookstore later.

If you have purchased this book as part of Dr. Wong's course, thank you. Do not forget to buy me a cup of coffee or drop me an e-mail if you get a job promotion later. However, if you have just downloaded this book from those illegal web sites and would like to keep it on your computer for future reference, you have three options:

1. Go to iUniverse's official web site to purchase a legitimate electronic copy. I have intentionally made the ebook version affordable (about US$10) so that my students can enjoy it without costing them an arm and a leg. Helping you understand the concept of intellectual properties is part of my teaching objectives.

2. Make a donation to your local charity or become a volunteer. I really mean it. If you absolutely do not want to pay the publisher for whatever reasons, please at least make a difference to help other people in your community.

3. Do nothing, if you think stealing is the right thing to do.

Have a great day and thanks for taking time to read my work. I wish you all the best in getting your first journal article published successfully!

Cheers,

Ken

References

Association of Business Schools. (2010). *ABS Academic Journal Quality Guide*. Retrieved from http://www.the-abs.org.uk/files// ABSalpha_intro_latest.pdf

Australian Business Deans Council. (2010). *ABDC Journal Ratings List*. Retrieved from http://www.abdc.edu.au/download. php?id=461294,245,1

Australian Research Council. (2010). *Ranked Journal List*. Retrieved from: http://www.arc.gov.au/xls/ERA2010_journal_title_list.xls

Chicago-Style Citation Quick Guide. (2010). *The Chicago Manual of Style Online*. Retrieved from http://www.chicagomanualofstyle.org/ tools_citationguide.html

Cranfield University. (2010). *Journal Recommendations for Academic Publication*. Retrieved from http://www.som.cranfield.ac.uk/som/ dinamic-content/media/SOM%20Journal%20Rankings%20 2010%20v1.05.pdf

Driscoll, S. and Gedymin, D. (2006). *Get Published!: Professionally, Affordably, Fast*. Bloomington, IN: iUniverse

Harzing, A-W. (2010). *Journal Quality List*. Retrieved from http:// www.harzing.com/jql.htm

Journal Rankings (2010). *SJR: Scientific Journal Rankings*. Retrieved from http://www.scimagojr.com/journalrank.php

Taylor & Francis (2010). *The Service Industries Journal - Instructions for Authors.* Retrieved from http://www.tandf.co.uk/journals/journal. asp?issn=0264-2069&linktype=44

The Basics of APA Style. (2010). *American Psychological Association - Learning APA Style.* Retrieved from http://www.apastyle.org/learn/ tutorials/basics-tutorial.aspx

Thomson Reuters (2010). *Journal Citation Reports.* Retrieved from http://thomsonreuters.com/products_services/science/science_ products/a-z/journal_citation_reports/

Using the Harvard style. (2010). *Imperial College London - Harvard Referencing Guide.* Retrieved from http://www3.imperial.ac.uk/ library/subjectsandsupport/referencemanagement/harvard

Wellington, J. (2003). *Getting Published: A Guide for Lecturers and Researchers.* London, UK: Routledge

Wong, K. (2011). *Avoiding Plagiarism: Write Better Papers in APA, Chicago, and Harvard Citation Styles.* Bloomington, IN: iUniverse

Index

A

B

C

D

E

F

G

H

I

J

Journal iii, iv, vii, viii, xiii, xv, 1, 2,
        3, 5, 6, 7, 8, 9, 11, 12, 13, 14,
        15, 16, 17, 18, 20, 21, 22, 23,
        25, 26, 27, 28, 29, 30, 31, 32,
        33, 34, 38, 39, 41, 42, 43, 44,
        45, 46, 47, 48, 49, 53, 54, 55,
        57, 58, 59, 60, 61, 62, 65, 66,
        67, 68

K

Keywords 18, 19, 20, 21, 24, 30, 34

L

LaTeX 31, 50
Legal Update 17, 22, 23
LISREL 13
Literature Review 19
Low Resolution Figure 37

M

Magazine 1, 25, 61, 62
MSN 44

O

Online Submission System 33, 34, 43,
        44, 45, 48
Open Access Journals 42
OpenOffice 31
Opinion Piece 17, 20
Original Research Article 12, 14, 17,
        18, 29
Oxford Comma 25

P

Page Assignment 53, 54, 68
Paper Submission 34, 41, 43, 60
Paper Title 28, 29, 34
PDF 26, 27, 38, 44, 54, 57
Photoshop 27, 37, 38, 39
Plagiarism viii, 32, 47, 65, 68

PowerPoint 21
Professional Magazines 61
ProQuest 30, 54
Publication Frequency 11, 12
Publication Llist 12, 15
Public Reaction 22

Q

Quality Assurance Checklist 34
Quality Control 25

R

Ranking 2, 5, 6, 12, 67
Readership Profile 12, 15, 16
Referencing 15, 18, 32, 35, 68
Rejection 47, 48, 63, 65
Rejoinder 17, 23, 24
research methodology 47
Research Methodology 18, 19, 47
Research Notes 17, 20
reviewer 65
Reviewer 2, 13, 14, 17, 46, 47, 48,
        57, 65
Revision 48
Running Head 29, 34

S

ScienceDirect 54
Screen Shots 37
72dpi 27, 28, 37, 38, 39
Skype 44
Straight Quotes 25

T

Tables 18, 26, 27, 34, 41, 42, 43, 44,
        50, 60, 62
Technical Notes 14, 17, 21
Tenure-track xv, 1, 2
Text Formatting 31
3-em dashes 25, 68
300dpi 27, 34, 38, 39
Trade Books 62

V

Volume 46, 53, 54, 62

W

Word Count 18, 30
WS_FTP 44